Beyond Love

A 12 Step Guide for Partners

Douglas Weiss, Ph.D.

Cover and Interior Design by Janelle Evangelides
Edited by Pauli Rancourt

Table of Contents

Introduction

The Twelve-Steps have helped millions of people recover from addictions such as alcohol, drugs, co-dependency, food, sex and many other addictions. This workbook takes you thoughtfully through your own personal healing from the affects of living with a sex addict. These steps will allow you to work at your own pace and with as many people from a partners Twelve-Step support group as you would like involved. Some Twelve-Step groups use this workbook for their step studies.

Our prayer is that you will experience hope and strength in your personal recovery journey, in all the areas of your life that his sex addiction has robbed you, so that you can once again experience the joy of living. Other resources that may help you in your recovery are available through Heart to Heart Counseling Center (see Appendix). May your healing be a gift you give to yourself and those you love.

For more information or to place orders, contact us at:

Heart to Heart Counseling Center
719-278-3708
www.sexaddict.com
heart2heart@xc.org

step one

We admitted we were powerless over our partner's sexual addiction
and that our lives had become unmanageable.

We is one of the most essential words in the Twelve-Steps. Often you may think you are the only one who is going through this crazy life-style with a sex addict. You may have consciously or unconsciously isolated yourself for years, but now you have come to a step that requires you to be part of a group.

What are some of the fears you have about becoming part of a recovering group?

1._____

2._____

3._____

What are some of the hopes and expectations you have as you enter into a group?

1._____

2._____

3._____

We also means that you are finally not alone. You now have other caring women who have suffered some of the same hurts and who carry similar fears. You are now finally understood. When the women in this group say, "I know what you mean and I know how you feel," you know you can believe them.

Have you come to a place where you shared some of your story and you felt accepted by a group?

Yes _____ No _____

If you answered yes to the previous question, briefly write this experience of being understood as it relates to your recovery.

_____

_____

_____

_____

If you believe you cannot write anything in the above space, list your reasons for not having opened up in the presence of other partners who are also healing from the affects of sexual addiction.

1._____

2._____

3._____

If you were able to identify any of these issues, take them to your group, discuss them and record your feedback here.

1._____

2._____

3._____

4._____

Admitted

Admitting can be a difficult thing to do. This can mean that in your sanest moments you will finally verbalize what you know to be true about yourself and your own situation. What are some of the things you have accepted about yourself as a partner of a sex addict?

1._____

_____

2._____

_____

3._____

_____

4._____

_____

How do you feel now that you have admitted these things to yourself?

I feel_____

_____

I feel _____

_____

_____

How long has it taken you to admit these things to yourself? _____

_____

Admitting can be one of the more difficult parts of your early recovery especially as you admit new and sometimes not so wonderful things about yourself. It seems to take even more energy and courage to admit something about yourself to others. Admitting is letting others know the truth about yourself.

What are some of the things you have admitted to yourself and to another person regarding being a partner of a sexual addict?

_____

_____

_____

_____

_____

Powerless

What are some definitions of power?

1. _____

2. _____

3. _____

What does the suffix "less" mean to you? (i.e. jobless, clueless, etc.)

1. _____

2. _____

3. _____

Combining your work in the previous two questions, what would your definition of "powerless" be?

_____

_____

_____

According to your definition are you able to accept being powerless?

Yes _____   No _____

What are some of the major things over which you are powerless?

1._____

2._____

3._____

4._____

How long have you been aware of your powerlessness in each of the areas you listed above?

1._____

2._____

3._____

4._____

If your behavior has not changed, what do you conclude about your current state of powerlessness?

_____

_____

How do you feel now that you are powerless over the sex addict in your life?

*I feel*_____

_____

_____

*I feel*_____

_____

_____

What is/are the first name(s) of the sex addict(s) that you are currently powerless over?

1._____

2._____

3._____

4._____

How has your behavior or attitudes changed toward the sex addict(s) over whom you are powerless?

1._____

2._____

3._____

If your behavior or attitudes have not changed toward the sex addict, what makes you believe you are powerless over him?

_____

_____

_____

On a scale from 1 to 10, how would you rate your powerlessness over the sex addict(s)? (10 being in control of, 1 being powerless over)

Name_____   1 2 3 4 5 6 7 8 9 10

Name_____   1 2 3 4 5 6 7 8 9 10

Name_____   1 2 3 4 5 6 7 8 9 10

Name_____   1 2 3 4 5 6 7 8 9 10

The Sex Addict

How did you find out that he was a sex addict?

_____

_____

_____

_____

How did this affect your relationship?

_____

_____

_____

_____

_____

_____

How did you feel when you found out that you need to heal from the affects of his addiction?

I felt _____

_____

I felt _____

_____

How do you feel toward your sex addict?

I feel _____

_____

I feel _____

_____

How do you feel toward other partners of sex addicts?

I feel _____

_____

I feel _____

_____

Are those feelings the same? If not, explain why.

_____

_____

_____

_____

_____

Unmanageable

Becoming anything is a process. How did your life become unmanageable? Give a brief historical account.

_____

_____

_____

_____

_____

_____

_____

What were the choices you made that caused your life to become unmanageable?

1._____

_____

2._____

_____

3._____

_____

4._____

_____

5._____

_____

In the following areas of your life, how did each area become unmanageable because of your relationship with the sex addict(s)?

Family Life

1._____

_____

2._____

_____

3._____

_____

🌸 Parenting

1._____

_____

2._____

_____

3._____

_____

🌸 Finances

1._____

_____

2._____

_____

3._____

_____

🌸 Friends

1._____

_____

2._____

_____

3._____

_____

🌸 Sexually

1._____

_____

2._____

_____

3._____

_____

Spiritually

1._____

_____

2._____

_____

3._____

_____

Emotionally

1._____

_____

2._____

_____

3._____

_____

Realizing that your life has become unmanageable is the first step toward healing. What were some of the turning points in your relationship with the sex addict(s) that made you aware your life was becoming unmanageable?

1._____

_____

2._____

_____

3._____

_____

As you look at these new revelations, you may wonder how you got to this point. Like many others you may have needed to hit a bottom or turning point. Do you feel you have hit this point? Why or why not?

_____

_____

_____

_____

_____

_____

_____

_____

_____

When a pessimist hears the word "bottom," she may feel hopeless or lost. If an optimist hears the same word she may feel hopeful and found. The optimist senses that there is only up from the bottom. This is also true when a partner discovers her powerlessness over her sex addict. What would be your definition of up from here in the following areas of your life?

Family life _____

_____

Parenting _____

_____

Financially _____

_____

Friends _____

_____

Sexually _____

_____

Spiritually _____

_____

*Emotionally*_____

_____

Take a moment and write short-term goals that could help you reach these "up-from-here" areas.

*Family life*_____

_____

_____

*Parenting*_____

_____

_____

*Financially*_____

_____

_____

*Friends*_____

_____

_____

*Sexually*_____

_____

_____

*Spiritually*_____

_____

_____

*Emotionally*_____

_____

_____

Was attending or starting a Partners or Twelve-Step meeting in your area one of your goals? Why or why not?

_____

_____

_____

_____

Was individual counseling by a professional who treats addiction issues included? Why or why not?

_____

_____

_____

_____

"We admitted we were powerless over the sex addict and that our lives had become unmanageable." Do you feel you have fully experienced Step One? Why or why not?

_____

_____

_____

_____

_____

What is the most significant thing you have learned about yourself in completing your Step One?

_____

_____

_____

_____

On a scale from 1-10 rate yourself on Step One.

1 2 3 4 5 6 7 8 9 10

Why? _____

_____

Feedback Form

The following space is provided for feedback ratings from your group in your step work. There is additional space as to why the rating is appropriate. You can use the feedback space also for reflection of your own work if you are working individually.

Name of Group Member _____Rating 1   2   3   4   5   6   7   8   9   10

Feedback _____

_____

_____

Name of Group Member _____Rating 1   2   3   4   5   6   7   8   9   10

Feedback _____

_____

_____

Name of Group Member _____Rating 1   2   3   4   5   6   7   8   9   10

Feedback _____

_____

_____

Name of Group Member _____Rating 1   2   3   4   5   6   7   8   9   10

Feedback _____

_____

_____

Name of Group Member _____Rating 1   2   3   4   5   6   7   8   9   10

Feedback _____

_____

_____

Name of Group Member _____Rating 1   2   3   4   5   6   7   8   9   10

Feedback _____

_____

_____

step two

Came to believe that a power greater
than ourselves could restore us to sanity.

This verb came is in the past tense. The word came implies the action has already happened. This means that in this step, you are receiving a report of a past event. Give significant, specific examples of coming to believe something.

1._____

2._____

3._____

4._____

What were some specific incidents that brought you to the point where you came to believe you were a partner of a sex addict?

1._____

2._____

3._____

4._____

How long did it take you to come to believe you were a partner of a sex addict?

_____

_____

_____

Was there a culminating event that caused you to believe you are a partner of a sex addict?

_____

_____

_____

Believe

How, in the previous examples, have your beliefs caused you to be different? (i.e., behavior or attitudes)

1._____

2._____

3._____

4._____

A Power Greater

Give any specific examples of coming to a point of belief in a greater power.

1._____

2._____

3._____

How has your coming to believe in this greater power affected your behavior in the past and present?

1._____

2._____

3._____

How has your coming to believe in this greater power affected your attitudes?

_____

_____

How has your coming to believe in this greater Power affected your relationships with:

Yourself

1._____

2._____

3._____

Significant Others

1._____

2._____

3._____

Family

1._____

2._____

3._____

Your Money

1._____

2._____

3._____

Your Sex Addict

1._____

2._____

3._____

When did this coming to believe in a greater power happen to you? (Approximate date)

_____

What happened exactly?

_____

_____

_____

_____

_____

_____

How would you define "greater?"

_____

_____

_____

How do you understand the word or concept of power?

_____

_____

_____

What are powers that are greater than yourself? Why?

1._____

2._____

3._____

4._____

What power are you selecting to be your greater power? (A power greater is singular-meaning only one.)

_____

_____

_____

What characteristics does your greater power have?

1._____

2._____

3._____

4._____

5._____

How do you know you can believe in this greater power?

1._____

2._____

3._____

How do you intend to utilize this greater power in your healing process?

_____

_____

_____

_____

Have you had a relationship with this greater power in your past? (Please explain.)

_____

_____

_____

_____

_____

If you had this relationship in the past, what led you away? _____

_____

_____

_____

How long have you been away from this relationship? _____

_____

How do you feel about being away from this greater power relationship?

*I feel*_____

_____

_____

Explain how you have experienced this greater power to be greater than all of yourself since you have chosen to heal?

1._____

_____

_____

2._____

_____

_____

3._____

_____

_____

Explain your current relationship with your greater power. _____

_____

_____

What activities or behaviors are involved in your relationship with your greater power?

1._____   4._____

2._____   5._____

3._____   6._____

How much time in a day or a week do you invest in your greater power relationship?

Day _____   Week _____

Could

What does it mean to you to believe that your greater power could do something to influence your healing process?

_____

_____

_____

In what way do you wish your higher power could be involved in your recovery?

1._____

2._____

3._____

4._____

5._____

What does the word restore mean to you?_____

_____

_____

_____

_____

In what ways would your greater power have to restore you in the following areas of your life?

Spiritually_____

_____

Family_____

_____

Parenting_____

_____

Financially_____

_____

Sexually_____

_____

Friendships_____

_____

Relationship with Yourself_____

_____

Your Future_____

_____

*Marriage/Significant Relationship*_____

_____

_____

In what ways has your greater power already been restoring you?_____

_____

_____

Notice that in this step it does not say "restore me to sanity," but it says the greater Power will "restore us to sanity." What does "us" in this step mean to you?

_____

_____

_____

_____

_____

_____

Sanity

List your behavior and attitudes which became insane during his sex addiction that you would now like your greater Power to restore.

1._____

2._____

3._____

4._____

5._____

6._____

How will you know when these attitudes or behaviors are restored?

1._____

2._____

3._____

4._____

5._____

6._____

7._____

"Came to believe that a Power greater than ourselves could restore us to sanity." Do you feel you have fully experienced Step Two? Why or Why not?

_____

_____

_____

_____

What is the most significant thing you have learned about yourself in completing Step Two?

_____

_____

_____

_____

In your own words, write what you believe to be the principle(s) of Step Two._____

_____

_____

On a scale from 1-10 rate yourself on Step Two.

1 2 3 4 5 6 7 8 9 10

Why?_____

_____

Feedback Form

The following space is provided for feedback ratings from your group in your step work. There is additional space as to why the rating is appropriate. You can use the feedback space also for reflection of your own work if you are working individually.

Name of Group Member _____Rating   1   2   3   4   5   6   7   8   9   10

Feedback _____

_____

_____

Name of Group Member _____Rating   1   2   3   4   5   6   7   8   9   10

Feedback _____

_____

_____

Name of Group Member _____Rating   1   2   3   4   5   6   7   8   9   10

Feedback _____

_____

_____

Name of Group Member _____Rating   1   2   3   4   5   6   7   8   9   10

Feedback _____

_____

_____

Name of Group Member _____Rating   1   2   3   4   5   6   7   8   9   10

Feedback _____

_____

_____

Name of Group Member _____Rating   1   2   3   4   5   6   7   8   9   10

Feedback _____

_____

_____

step three

Made a decision to turn our wills and our loves over
to the care of God, as we understood God.

Made

Made is the past tense of the verb make. Make can be defined as a process involving effort to build or construct something. There are processes which are involved in making a decision. What are some of the events that have brought you to the point of deciding to turn your life and will over to God as you understand Him?

1._____

_____

2._____

_____

3._____

_____

As a partner, you have turned your will and your life over to various things, persons or beliefs. List the things, persons or beliefs to which you have turned over your will and life in the past. (Be specific.)

1._____

_____

2._____

_____

3._____

_____

4._____

_____

Have you made decisions in the past to turn your life over to God? (i.e., If you get me out of this one...) List them.

1._____

_____

2._____

_____

3._____

_____

Have you had moments of desperation while in a relationship with a sex addict, when you cried out to God to take control over your life?

1._____

_____

2._____

_____

3._____

_____

4._____

_____

How is this decision different from previous decisions?_____

_____

_____

Since made is in the past tense, explain how you have been affected since turning your will and life over to the care of God, especially in your healing process. (What has changed? What are you doing differently?)

1._____

_____

2._____

_____

3._____

_____

4._____

_____

Making a major decision in your life often requires time and much thought. What were other major decisions you made in the past? How long did it take to make them? (Marriage/divorce/business choices)

1._____

_____

2._____

_____

3._____

_____

4._____

_____

In the above cases, where were you when you made that final decision?

1._____

_____

2._____

_____

3._____

_____

4._____

_____

If Step Three is thought through carefully, it is probably a decision much like marriage or choosing a vocation. How much time have you put into this step up at this point?_____

_____

_____

Can you identify a specific moment or culminating event that marks when you initially did your Step Three? If so, please explain. _____

_____

_____

_____

_____

If the previous answer is no, explain how you know you have done your Step Three. _____

_____

_____

What areas in your life are you most reluctant to have God in charge of?

List these areas and explain.   Why?

1._____   1._____

2._____   2._____

3._____   3._____

4._____   4._____

5._____   5._____

Explain how you will allow God to have your will and life in these areas.

1._____

_____

_____

2._____

_____

_____

3._____

_____

_____

4._____

_____

5._____

_____

_____

Care

What other words come to mind when you hear the word care as it pertains to the "care of God?"

1._____   3._____

2._____   4._____

How has God cared for you since you have given your will and life to Him?

1._____

_____

_____

2._____

_____

_____

3._____

_____

Has God, as you understand Him, demonstrated His care for you before you made this decision? If so, list three times.

1._____

_____

2._____

_____

3._____

_____

God

God can be a scary reality to some during the healing process. On this page, explain God as you understand Him.

_____

_____

_____

_____

_____

_____

In Step Two, you chose a Power greater than yourself. How did God differ from this greater Power concept?

_____

_____

_____

What are characteristics you like and dislike about God?

Like?   *Dislike?*

1._____   1._____

2._____   2._____

3._____   3._____

4._____   4._____

5._____   5._____

Does God have the freedom to be the final authority in these areas of your life?

Socially	Yes	No		*Job*	Yes	No
Finances	Yes	No		*Parenting*	Yes	No
Marriage	Yes	No		*Recovery*	Yes	No
Dating	Yes	No		*Spiritually*	Yes	No
Sexually	Yes	No		*Other Addictions*	Yes	No

Why do you trust God with your will and life? _____

_____

_____

_____

_____

_____

What do you consider to be your will? _____

_____

_____

What do you consider to be your life? _____

_____

Why? _____

_____

What percentage are you turning over? _____

Will _____% Life _____% Why? _____

_____

As We Understand Him

We may all learn more about God as we live in a community of people trying to give their wills and lives over to the care of God. Ask four people who have been in recovery for longer than a year to describe "God as they understand Him," as He is active in their lives now. Record their responses.

1. _____

_____

2. _____

_____

3. _____

_____

4. _____

_____

How do you presently practice learning more about God as you understand Him?

1._____

2._____

3._____

4._____

List events that demonstrate you having turned your will over to God instead of allowing self-will to rule.

1._____

_____

2._____

_____

3._____

_____

4._____

_____

In what way have you turned your life over to God in these areas?

Family_____

_____

_____

Marriage_____

_____

_____

Dating_____

_____

_____

Sexually _____

_____

_____

_____

Job _____

_____

_____

_____

Future _____

_____

_____

Financially _____

_____

Recovery _____

_____

_____

Socially _____

_____

_____

Below or on a separate piece of paper, write a letter to God as you understand Him.

Dear God,

_____

_____

_____

_____

_____

_____

_____

_____

_____

_____

_____

_____

_____

_____

_____

_____

_____

_____

_____

_____

_____

_____

_____

_____

_____

_____

_____

_____

"Made a decision to turn our will and lives over to the care of God as we understand Him." What is the most significant thing you have learned about yourself while completing Step Three?

_____

_____

_____

_____

What is the most significant thing you learned about yourself in completing your Step Three?

_____

_____

_____

_____

On a scale from 1-10 rate yourself on Step Three.

1 2 3 4 5 6 7 8 9 10

Why? _____

_____

Feedback Form

The following space is provided for feedback ratings from your group in your step work. There is additional space as to why the rating is appropriate. You can use the feedback space also for reflection of your own work if you are working individually.

Name of Group Member _____Rating 1   2   3   4   5   6   7   8   9   10

Feedback _____

_____

_____

Name of Group Member _____Rating 1   2   3   4   5   6   7   8   9   10

Feedback _____

_____

_____

Name of Group Member _____Rating 1   2   3   4   5   6   7   8   9   10

Feedback _____

_____

_____

Name of Group Member _____Rating 1   2   3   4   5   6   7   8   9   10

Feedback _____

_____

_____

Name of Group Member _____Rating 1   2   3   4   5   6   7   8   9   10

Feedback _____

_____

_____

Name of Group Member _____Rating 1   2   3   4   5   6   7   8   9   10

Feedback _____

_____

_____

step four

Made a searching and fearless moral inventory of ourselves.

Made

In Step Four, you are to have made (past tense) a moral inventory of yourself. Most likely, in the midst of your partner's addiction, you did not have the clarity of mind or sanity to distinguish between the morality or immorality of a particular behavior or belief. It is now necessary to do so.

List strengths and weaknesses you have in the spiritual areas of your life.

Strengths

1._____
2._____
3._____
4._____

Weaknesses

1._____
2._____
3._____
4._____

List strengths and weaknesses you have in financial areas of your life.

Strengths

1._____
2._____
3._____
4._____

Weaknesses

1._____
2._____
3._____
4._____

List strengths and weaknesses you have in your relationships in general.

Strengths

1._____
2._____

Weaknesses

1._____
2._____

3._____   3._____

4._____   4._____

List strengths and weaknesses you have in significant male-female relationships.

Strengths   Weaknesses

1._____   1._____

2._____   2._____

3._____   3._____

4._____   4._____

List strengths and weaknesses you have as an employee.

Strengths   Weaknesses

1._____   1._____

2._____   2._____

3._____   3._____

4._____   4._____

List strengths and weaknesses you have in relating to your:

Mother

Strengths   Weaknesses

1._____   1._____

2._____   2._____

3._____   3._____

4._____   4._____

Father

Strengths

1._____

2._____

3._____

4._____

Weaknesses

1._____

2._____

3._____

4._____

Siblings

Strengths

1._____

2._____

3._____

4._____

Weaknesses

1._____

2._____

3._____

4._____

Yourself

Strengths

1._____

2._____

3._____

4._____

Weaknesses

1._____

2._____

3._____

4._____

Those less fortunate

Strengths

1._____

2._____

Weaknesses

1._____

2._____

3._____   3._____

4._____   4._____

🌸 Authorities

Strengths   Weaknesses

1._____   1._____

2._____   2._____

3._____   3._____

4._____   4._____

The above assessments will give you an idea of how positive or less than positive you have been in your behavior or beliefs toward yourself and others. There is yet another inventory you must fearlessly take in this step: an inventory that is a deliberate search for additional moral information about yourself.

You will need to be courageous as you look at your strengths, shortcomings, or losses that you have had up to this point in your life. These losses may not have been intentional but have, nevertheless, caused loss (i.e., death or divorce). The loss of innocence by being sexually abused or loss of confidence from not being able to make decisions while growing up are also significant in this inventory.

🌸 Losses

In the appropriate space, place your losses and/or abuses, neglect, etc., in one column and the strengths of that period in your life in another column. (Be specific: include what happened, with whom, feelings then and now about the event.) Your strengths will be positive experiences you have had that you still draw strength from today.

Age 1-6 (i.e., physical, sexual, emotional abuse; divorce; death of a loved one; losses; being adopted or abandoned by a parent; other significant events, positive or negative)

Losses   Strengths

_____   _____

_____   _____

_____   _____

_____   _____

_____   _____

_____   _____

_____   _____

Age 7-12 (i.e., school problems; physical, sexual, emotional abuse; other significant events, positive or negative)

Losses

_____

_____

_____

_____

_____

_____

_____

Strengths

_____

_____

_____

_____

_____

_____

_____

Age 13-15, (i.e., significant events, positive or negative, including alcohol/drug or sexual experimentation)

Losses

_____

_____

_____

_____

_____

_____

_____

Strengths

_____

_____

_____

_____

_____

_____

_____

Age 16-25, (i.e., significant events, positive or negative; sexually activity; rapes; school problems; etc.)

Losses

_____

_____

_____

_____

_____

_____

_____

Strengths

_____

_____

_____

_____

_____

_____

_____

Age 26-35, (i.e., alcohol/drug patterns; male/female relationships; marriages; divorces; children; sexual activity; traumas; deaths; etc.)

Losses

_____

_____

_____

_____

_____

_____

Strengths

_____

_____

_____

_____

_____

_____

Age 36-45, (i.e., alcohol/drug patterns; male/female relationships; divorces; children; sexual activity; traumas; deaths; etc.)

Losses

_____

_____

_____

_____

_____

_____

_____

Strengths

_____

_____

_____

_____

_____

_____

_____

Age 46-55, (i.e., alcohol/drug patterns; male/female relationships; marriages; divorces; children; sexual activity; traumas; deaths; etc.)

Losses

_____

_____

_____

_____

_____

_____

Strengths

_____

_____

_____

_____

_____

_____

Age 56-65, (i.e., alcohol/drug patterns; male/female relationships; marriages; divorces; children; sexual activity; traumas; deaths; etc.)

Losses | Strengths

\
\
\
\
\
\
\

Age 66+, (i.e., alcohol/drug patterns; male/female relationships; marriages; divorces; children; sexual activity; traumas; deaths; etc.)

Losses | Strengths

\
\
\
\
\
\
\

Have you been 100% honest in writing down the losses of which you are aware of?

Yes _____ No _____

Are there specific things you were too ashamed to write down at this point in your healing process?

Yes _____ No _____

Ourselves

Notice again the plurality of the word "ourselves." The recovery community can help you learn much about yourself. Contact four recovering people who have completed Step Four and ask them what they have learned about themselves. Record answers in the space provided below using their first names only.

1. _____

_____

2. _____

_____

3. _____

_____

4. _____

What have you learned in this step about "*ourselves*"?

1. _____

_____

2. _____

_____

3. _____

_____

4. _____

What specifically have you learned about yourself?

1. _____

_____

2. _____

_____

3. _____

_____

"Made a searching and fearless moral inventory of ourselves." Do you feel you have fully experienced Step Four? Why or why not?

_____

_____

_____

_____

What is the most significant thing you have learned about yourself in completing your Step Four?

_____

_____

_____

_____

How do you feel about completing this step?

*I feel*_____

_____

_____

How do you feel about yourself?

*I feel*_____

_____

_____

On a scale from 1-10 rate yourself on Step Four.

1   2   3   4   5   6   7   8   9   10

*Why?*_____

_____

Feedback Form

The following space is provided for feedback ratings from your group in your step work. There is additional space as to why the rating is appropriate. You can use the feedback space also for reflection of your own work if you are working individually.

Name of Group Member _____Rating 1 2 3 4 5 6 7 8 9 10

Feedback _____

_____

_____

Name of Group Member _____Rating 1 2 3 4 5 6 7 8 9 10

Feedback _____

_____

_____

Name of Group Member _____Rating 1 2 3 4 5 6 7 8 9 10

Feedback _____

_____

_____

Name of Group Member _____Rating 1 2 3 4 5 6 7 8 9 10

Feedback _____

_____

_____

Name of Group Member _____Rating 1 2 3 4 5 6 7 8 9 10

Feedback _____

_____

_____

Name of Group Member _____Rating 1 2 3 4 5 6 7 8 9 10

Feedback _____

_____

_____

step five

Admitted to God, to ourselves, and to another human
being the exact nature of our wrongs.

In your journey so far, you have been either reunited with or introduced, for the first time, to God as you understand Him. This will help to admit to Him the exact nature of your wrongs. The journey through Step Four gave you some awareness of yourself. Step Five will further aid you in your understanding of yourself.

Admitting

Admitting can often be the hardest thing to do. Are there reasons you would like to not entirely admit the exact nature of your wrongs? (i.e., fear of being rejected if others knew or sexual shame) List these.

1._____

_____

2._____

_____

3._____

_____

If you have written something in the spaces above, get feedback from recovering people who have already gone through Step Five. How did they deal with this?

1._____

_____

2._____

_____

3._____

_____

If you did not write anything for the previous question, ask three recovering people who have done their Step Five what some of their experiences were that they had in completing this step.

Ask these same three people what feelings they had after doing their Step Five.

1._____

_____

2._____

_____

3._____

_____

Now you come to an hour of reckoning within yourself. Often, to your own harm, you continuously carry with you a list of things you have done wrong. It is time to record this list on paper.

Make a list of people you are aware of that you have wronged and their relationship to you. Write exactly what you did wrong to each of them. (If more than one time, indicate this.) Remember to list exactly each wrong done.

Name	Relationship	Wrong Done

_____   _____   _____

_____   _____   _____

_____   _____   _____

Now that you have looked at wrongs from a relational point of view, let's look at them chronologically. Remember to include in chronological order any abuses (physical, sexual, emotional). Use Step Four to help you.

In the space provided, list the names of people you have wronged and a brief explanation of the exact wrong doing.

Include those on previous pages.

Age 1-6,

_____

_____

_____

Age 7-12,

_____

_____

_____

_____

_____

_____

Age 13-18,

_____

_____

_____

_____

_____

_____

_____

_____

Age 19-25.

_____

_____

_____

_____

_____

_____

_____

_____

Age 26-35.

_____

_____

_____

_____

_____

_____

_____

_____

_____

Age 36-45.

_____

_____

_____

_____

_____

Age 46-55.

Age 56-65.

Age 66+,

_____
_____
_____
_____
_____
_____
_____
_____
_____
_____
_____
_____

Now that you have listed the exact nature of your wrongs, you will need to admit them to another human being. What type of person do you think this human being should be?

1._____

2._____

3._____

Do you have someone picked out? If not, why not?_____

_____

If so, what is the person's first name and relationship to you?_____

_____

When did you communicate verbally all the information you wrote down in this step to someone of the same sex?

Date _____/_____/_____

Did you hold anything back that you were too embarrassed to tell?

Yes _____   No _____

If so, list them and make a second appointment with this significant person.

1._____

2._____

3._____

"Admitted to God, to ourselves, and to another human being the exact nature of our wrongs." Do you feel you have fully experienced Step Five? Why or why not?

_____

_____

_____

_____

What is the most significant thing you have learned about yourself in completing your Step Five?

_____

_____

_____

_____

On a scale from 1-10 rate yourself on Step Five.

1 2 3 4 5 6 7 8 9 10

Why? _____

_____

Feedback Form

The following space is provided for feedback ratings from your group in your step work. There is additional space as to why the rating is appropriate. You can use the feedback space also for reflection of your own work if you are working individually.

Name of Group Member _____Rating 1   2   3   4   5   6   7   8   9   10

Feedback _____

_____

_____

Name of Group Member _____Rating 1   2   3   4   5   6   7   8   9   10

Feedback _____

_____

_____

Name of Group Member _____Rating 1   2   3   4   5   6   7   8   9   10

Feedback _____

_____

_____

Name of Group Member _____Rating 1   2   3   4   5   6   7   8   9   10

Feedback _____

_____

_____

Name of Group Member _____Rating 1   2   3   4   5   6   7   8   9   10

Feedback _____

_____

_____

Name of Group Member _____Rating 1   2   3   4   5   6   7   8   9   10

Feedback _____

_____

_____

step six

Were entirely ready to have God remove all these defects of character.

Entirely

When you think of the word entirely, many pictures may come to mind. One of the most vivid pictures is that of a sprinter with her foot on the block and hands in the dirt in front of the white line, while looking at the gun, ready to go off. This is an appropriate picture for entirely. Entirely is 100% ready to do something. Many partners in the past have been entirely ready to destroy their lives for a relationship with the sex addict to avoid dealing with pain from the past. Now you have come to another point in your life where you are entirely ready, after completing Steps One through Five, to do something to further better yourself.

What are some of the words you think of when you think of the word entirely?

1._____

2._____

3._____

What are some of the feelings you have when you think of the word entirely?

I feel_____

_____

_____

I feel_____

_____

_____

What are a two examples in your life when you were entirely ready to do something? (Be specific)

_____

_____

What were some of the major instances that made you entirely ready?

_____

_____

_____

To Have God

Who has God become to you during your journey through Steps One through Five?

_____

_____

_____

What roles is He filling in your life?

_____

_____

_____

What feelings do you have toward God at this point?

_____

_____

_____

Why do you think that you need "to have God" involved in this part of your healing process?

_____

_____

_____

How have you relied upon God in the past?

_____

_____

_____

What aspects or characteristics of God are you relying upon to help in the process of removing your defects of character?

_____

_____

_____

Remove

Remove is another word in your healing process that can mean something very painful to you as a partner. Remove in the form of an analogy can mean "to remove weeds from your grass, pulling them up" or in another picture to "remove a tumor that in the future could kill you."

What are some words or phrases that come to mind when you think of the word remove?

1._____

2._____

3._____

4._____

What are some of the feelings you have when you think of something being removed from you?

I feel _____

_____

_____

I feel _____

_____

_____

What are some of the things that have been removed from you up to this point in your recovery?

1._____

2._____

3._____

How do you feel about these things being removed?

_____

_____

_____

How has God been involved in the removal process?

_____

_____

_____

All

All means quite a bit to anyone in the healing process.

What are some words that come to your mind when you think of the word all?

1._____

2._____

3._____

What percentage is all? _____%

What percentage do you want all to mean when you talk about removing your defects of character?
_____%

Defects

What are some of the defects that you have seen in your past?

Age 1-12.

1._____

2._____

3._____

4._____

5._____

Age 13-20.

1._____

2._____

3._____

4._____

5._____

Age 21-30.

1._____

2._____

3._____

4._____

5._____

Age 31-40.

1._____

2._____

3._____

4._____

5._____

Age 41-50.

1._____

2._____

3._____

4._____

5._____

Age 51-60.

1._____

2._____

3._____

4._____

5._____

Age 61 +

1._____

2._____

3._____

4._____

5._____

What are some of the defects you have in relating to:

Yourself?

1._____

2._____

3._____

Your family of origin?

1._____

2._____

3._____

Your spouse or significant other?

1._____

2._____

3._____

Children?

1._____

2._____

3._____

Your employer?

1._____

2._____

3._____

Financially?

1._____

2._____

3._____

Socially?

1._____

2._____

3._____

Spiritually?

1._____

2._____

3._____

At this point, take some time and compile a full list of these defects of character.

Identify the length of time each character defect has been in your life. Next, looking at these defects of character, what percentage are you ready to have God remove each of these defects? Write a percentage by each one.

Example:

Defects	Length Of Time	Percentage
Self willed	32 years	80-90%

Take time with each one of these character defects and write a paragraph on a separate piece of paper about what life would be like without this defect in your life. Use the below lines to summarize your writings.

_____

_____

_____

_____

_____

_____

_____

_____

_____

_____

Write the character defects that you are 100% ready to have God remove. Only write down the ones that you are totally ready to have God remove. In other words, if God could take this defect from you, you would let him have it and not want to take it back from Him?

_____   _____   _____

_____   _____   _____

_____   _____   _____

_____   _____   _____

Have a time of prayer and meditation regarding your defects of character that you were not previously ready to have God remove. Now write the date that you became entirely ready for Him to remove all these defects.

_____/_____/_____

Character is what you are as a person and character defects are carbon spots that mar your character. These are the things that are important for you to identify. If you know where the spots are, you can surely ask God to help you with them.

This ends your journey on Step Six. Step Six simply asks you to become entirely ready to have God remove all your defects of character. You have listed your defects and thought through what it would be like to have these defects removed.

"Were entirely ready to have God remove all these defects of character." Do you feel you have experienced Step Six? Why or why not?

_____

_____

_____

_____

What is the most significant thing you have learned about yourself in completing your Step Six?

_____

_____

_____

On a scale from 1-10 rate yourself on Step Six.

1 2 3 4 5 6 7 8 9 10

Why? _____

_____

Feedback Form

The following space is provided for feedback ratings from your group in your step work. There is additional space as to why the rating is appropriate. You can use the feedback space also for reflection of your own work if you are working individually.

Name of Group Member _____Rating 1   2   3   4   5   6   7   8   9   10

Feedback _____

_____

_____

Name of Group Member _____Rating 1   2   3   4   5   6   7   8   9   10

Feedback _____

_____

_____

Name of Group Member _____Rating 1   2   3   4   5   6   7   8   9   10

Feedback _____

_____

_____

Name of Group Member _____Rating 1   2   3   4   5   6   7   8   9   10

Feedback _____

_____

_____

Name of Group Member _____Rating 1   2   3   4   5   6   7   8   9   10

Feedback _____

_____

_____

Name of Group Member _____Rating 1   2   3   4   5   6   7   8   9   10

Feedback _____

_____

_____

step seven

Humbly asked God to remove our shortcomings.

Humbly

Humbly can be defined as a disposition, an attitude, a reverence, or a submissiveness. I can remember a couple of instances during my school years when I was called into the principal's office and felt humble while waiting to go into his office, because I knew the principal could impact my life. He could have an affect on me and having the authority to do something, either positively or negatively, I was at his mercy. This feeling of humbleness was likely also experienced in your life.

What are some of the experiences you have had that have caused you to feel humble?

1._____

2._____

3._____

What are feelings that accompanied you in those experiences when you were humbled?

I felt _____

_____

_____

I felt _____

_____

_____

I felt _____

_____

_____

When was the last time you were in an experience like that?

_____

_____

_____

Asked

There is an old saying "you have not because you asked not." This is also true when it comes to your healing in Step Seven. Many have never honestly looked or fully looked at their character defects or limitations. For the first time, you have an intelligent list to ask from.

What are some of the things that you have asked of God before and you have received them?

1. _____

2. _____

3. _____

Many times, it takes what some people call "faith," "trust", or even "hope" in asking. Some of you have felt or feel so desperate and full of despair because of shortcomings you have that feel like there is no way out of. Now you come to a point where you can ask. Asking doesn't always mean it is going to happen the way you want it to, or that you are going to be in control of the procedure. Bet let's go ahead and look at the possibility of asking.

What are some of the character defects you identified in Step Six that you would like to ask to be removed?

1. _____

2. _____

3. _____

4. _____

5. _____

6. _____

7. _____

8. _____

9. _____

10. _____

Him

Him refers to God. At this point in your recovery, God is the only power greater than "ourselves" according to Step Three.

What are some of the aspects of God you are clinging to as you ask Him to do these things for you?

_____

_____

_____

_____

Have you experienced these characteristics before in your relationship with God? If so, how?

1._____

2._____

3._____

4._____

5._____

Remove

We talked about remove in Step Six. This is where you ask for it to actually happen. You are beyond "entirely ready." You are at the physician's table and asking Him to make an incision and remove the cancer and the things that ail you. You are asking Him to cut deep into your mind and will and remove. During this surgical procedure, there are a variety of experiences that you may have.

What are some of the experiences you are anticipating to happen?

1._____

2._____

3._____

Have you had any experience with God removing anything else in your life?

Yes _____   No _____

If so, explain what and how He removed it.

_____

_____

Did you believe or did you foreknow that He would do the removal the way He did?

Yes _____ No _____

It is true that the removal process is somewhat of a mystery. Who would think that to create patience you would experience situations that would cause you to become patient? Who would think that in the process of becoming kind, you would have to actually change or behave in a new way?

Many of the processes that God is going to use in your life are not in your control, nor should they be. The removing is not your doing. It is clear that you are asking someone else to do something much like going to a surgeon's office and asking them to operate to fix something. You don't have the insight or the education that the surgeon has, nor would you want it. You just have to trust that they have it and can do what you are asking them to do.

Have you seen God remove things in other people's lives?

Yes _____ No _____

Was He successful in these surgeries?

Yes _____ No _____

What are some of the feelings you have of God being in control of removing the things that you have listed as being 100% ready to remove in Step Six?

I feel _____

_____

_____

I feel _____

_____

_____

Our

Our is a great word in the Twelve-Steps. It means that there is more than just one person who has gone through this and that you are not the only one who has to. You are not alone, nor will you ever be.

Who are some of the people you know who have done their Step Seven?

1. _____

2. _____

3. _____

4. _____

What are some of their experiences after going through a Step Seven? List these.

1._____

_____

2._____

_____

3._____

_____

4._____

Shortcomings

Shortcomings are the same things as defects. They are the carbon spots or issues you have identified in Step Six.

Review your Step Six and look carefully over the defects that you said you were 100% ready to have God remove. On a separate sheet of paper, write out your prayers to ask God to remove one character defect at a time. Don't rob yourself and try to clump them all together. Ask Him to take His knowledge and ways to systematically remove them and give Him full permission to rank them in His order. He sees the most important and viable issues. It is much like surgery. Sometimes the surgeon has to prioritize what is going on within the system. If someone has been shot, he has to look past something else to get to what is primary. Allow God to prioritize as He removes these aspects of your character defects.

This page is a space that will be used over the next 12 months. In the table below, write your defects in the left column, and in the middle column, list the date you prayed for each defect to be removed. Write on a calendar or set an appointment in your phone to come back in a year to review your progress. Make a note at the one year mark and see how much work God has done.

Defect	Date Prayed For Removal	My One Year Progress Note

"Humbly asked Him to remove our shortcomings." Do you feel you have fully experienced Step Seven? Why or why not?

_____

_____

_____

_____

What is the most significant thing you have learned about yourself in completing your Step Seven?

_____

_____

_____

On a scale from 1-10 rate yourself on Step Seven.

1 2 3 4 5 6 7 8 9 10

Why? _____

_____

Feedback Form

The following space is provided for feedback ratings from your group in your step work. There is additional space as to why the rating is appropriate. You can use the feedback space also for reflection of your own work if you are working individually.

Name of Group Member _____ Rating 1 2 3 4 5 6 7 8 9 10

Feedback _____

_____

_____

Name of Group Member _____ Rating 1 2 3 4 5 6 7 8 9 10

Feedback _____

_____

_____

Name of Group Member _____ Rating 1 2 3 4 5 6 7 8 9 10

Feedback _____

_____

_____

Name of Group Member _____ Rating 1 2 3 4 5 6 7 8 9 10

Feedback _____

_____

_____

Name of Group Member _____ Rating 1 2 3 4 5 6 7 8 9 10

Feedback _____

_____

_____

Name of Group Member _____ Rating 1 2 3 4 5 6 7 8 9 10

Feedback _____

_____

_____

step eight

Made a list of all persons we had harmed, and became
willing to make amends to them all.

Made A List

Throughout the Twelve-Steps, many have made decisions to turn their lives over to the care of God, and they have also made searching and fearless inventories. Now you will take time, energy, and creativity to make a list.

Of All Persons

Again, we're confronted with the word all. All means 100% in this case. This includes people in your past and present that you have related to.

We

We, again, is very relieving because you are not the only person who has caused others harm. Most who have caused harm through personal issues have dealt with the pain and shame from the past. Harm is a tricky word for many and that is why it is printed in Step Eight. It is now time to look at what you may have done in your life that has caused harm to others. Let's take a sober moment to think about this issue. You may want to consider praying and asking God to help you make this list.

Make this list chronologically, according to those you have harmed. This is the part in your Step Four where you listed the good, the bad, and the ugly (the good are good things, the bad are bad things you were responsible for, and the ugly are bad things done to you that you were not responsible for). This would be a good time to go back to Step Four and look over the things you have done (the bad) and the people you have harmed. Make a list of these people. Use additional paper if necessary.

Age 1-12,

_____   _____

_____   _____

_____   _____

_____   _____

_____   _____

Age 13-20,

_____   _____
_____   _____
_____   _____
_____   _____

Age 21-30,

_____   _____
_____   _____
_____   _____
_____   _____
_____   _____

Age 31-40,

_____   _____
_____   _____
_____   _____
_____   _____
_____   _____

Age 41-50,

_____   _____
_____   _____
_____   _____
_____   _____
_____   _____

Age 51-60,

_____   _____
_____   _____
_____   _____
_____   _____

Age 61 +

_____   _____
_____   _____
_____   _____
_____   _____
_____   _____

Take time to compile a list of these people who you have caused pain to more than once.

_____   _____
_____   _____
_____   _____
_____   _____
_____   _____
_____   _____
_____   _____
_____   _____
_____   _____
_____   _____

And

And is a great conjunction. I am glad that you didn't stop at just making the list. If you did, it would possibly be too painful to bear.

How do you feel about making your list?

I feel _____
_____
_____

I feel _____
_____
_____

Became

This is a process. It takes time. Give yourself permission to become as it relates to this Step Eight, and become willing to make amends. This is similar to Step Four and Five where you are reckoning a part of yourself. How did you feel after Step Five?

I felt _____

_____

_____

I felt _____

_____

_____

Willing

We have talked about being willing indirectly in Step Six when we talked about being "entirely ready." Willing means that you are, regardless of emotion, willing to submit or comply to what needs to be done. This doesn't mean that you are going to do it yet, but simply that you are willing. For those of you who exercise, it is similar to laying in bed and at some point becoming willing and then moving into the direction of going to exercise. You don't just arrive at the gym but begin moving in that direction.

What are your experiences in becoming willing during your Twelve Step process?

1._____

2._____

3._____

What were the results of this willingness?

1._____

2._____

3._____

Making Amends

An amend is making something right again, to restore or try to mend something that has been broken. Many of you will do this as you move from your Step Eight to your Step Nine. Part of Step Eight is that you become willing to make that step and mend what has been broken, acknowledging your responsibility in the breaking of it.

To Them All

What percentage is all? _____%

Place what percentage of how willing you are to make an amend to these people listed in the next page.

20%   50%   100%

Example: Friend   80%

Make a list of these people again. Use additional paper if necessary.

1._____	_____%	11._____	_____%
2._____	_____%	12._____	_____%
3._____	_____%	13._____	_____%
4._____	_____%	14._____	_____%
5._____	_____%	15._____	_____%
6._____	_____%	16._____	_____%
7._____	_____%	17._____	_____%
8._____	_____%	18._____	_____%
9._____	_____%	19._____	_____%
10._____	_____%	20._____	_____%

Use this list, praying regularly as you consider these individuals, until you become willing to make amends to them all.

Write below the date when you became 100% willing to make amends to every person on this list.

_____

"Made a list of all people we have harmed and became willing to make amends to them all." Do you feel you have fully experienced Step Eight? Why or why not?

_____

_____

_____

_____

What is the most significant thing you have learned about yourself in completing your Step Eight?

_____

_____

_____

On a scale from 1-10 rate yourself on Step Eight.

1 2 3 4 5 6 7 8 9 10

Why? _____

_____

Feedback Form

The following space is provided for feedback ratings from your group in your step work. There is additional space as to why the rating is appropriate. You can use the feedback space also for reflection of your own work if you are working individually.

Name of Group Member _____Rating 1   2   3   4   5   6   7   8   9   10

Feedback _____

_____

_____

Name of Group Member _____Rating 1   2   3   4   5   6   7   8   9   10

Feedback _____

_____

_____

Name of Group Member _____Rating 1   2   3   4   5   6   7   8   9   10

Feedback _____

_____

_____

Name of Group Member _____Rating 1   2   3   4   5   6   7   8   9   10

Feedback _____

_____

_____

Name of Group Member _____Rating 1   2   3   4   5   6   7   8   9   10

Feedback _____

_____

_____

Name of Group Member _____Rating 1   2   3   4   5   6   7   8   9   10

Feedback _____

_____

_____

step nine

Made direct amends to such people wherever possible, except
when to do so would injure them or others.

Made

This is the last made in your Twelve-Step journey and it may be the most painful one. Now you
will turn your energies, creativity, and time into making one more thing, and that is a direct amends
to those you have harmed.

Direct

What are some words you think of when you think of the word direct?

1._____

2._____

3._____

What are some of the words opposite of the direct?

1._____

2._____

3._____

How do you feel about these opposite words when someone is behaving that way toward you?

I feel_____

_____

_____

I feel_____

_____

_____

How do you feel toward someone who is being direct toward you?

I feel _____

_____

_____

I feel _____

_____

_____

Direct is definitely the straightest line between any two points. Your past may be vague, rationalized, shamed and blamed, and you may have avoided many of your behaviors. Some of your own defense mechanisms were to blame others for your behaviors. Some were rationalizations of why you did it and why you weren't responsible. Some were minimizations where you thought "it didn't hurt that badly" and you were not able to see the damage that you had done in other people's lives. These defense mechanisms helped you quite a bit to stay unhealthy but they have no help for you in your healing process. Let's discuss what direct means.

In recovery, as it relates to these amends, here is the best formula for direct.

1. Face to face contact: Talk to the person, face to face, and have a discussion regarding what you have done that has caused them harm. This is the most direct amend that can be made in a relationship. This is by far the best method of being direct with your amends.

2. Phone calls: If the person is too far to travel to in order to make a direct amend, then a phone call can suffice as a second most direct amend.

3. Letter: For the person who does not have a phone, or can not be reached in any other manner, a letter is your least direct amend.

 Amends

Amends is a process of bringing two things that are broken back together or at least to a point of contact. You are not responsible to restore the relationship, that takes two. An amend is only you cleaning your side of the street. It does not minimize, rationalize or blame any one for the behavior you did that caused pain. It is you looking fully at the pain that you caused another human being and acknowledging that pain to them. It is asking them to forgive you and advance in the relationship as they wish to. You are not responsible for their forgiveness. You are only 100% responsible to make the amend to them.

Such People

Make a list of the people from Step Eight and in the columns provided, check off those you can do face to face amends to. Check off who you can make phone calls to. Lastly, check off those you will write a letter to.

Name	Face to Face	Phone Call	Letter
1.			
2.			
3.			
4.			
5.			
6.			
7.			
8.			
9.			
10.			
11.			
12.			
13.			
14.			
15.			
16.			
17.			
18.			
19.			
20.			

Wherever Possible

In the 1930's when the steps were written, wherever possible was more limited than today. Today, wherever possible is almost everywhere due to planes and/or technology where you can reach anyone in the world. Wherever possible is also acknowledging the fact that not everyone who you owe an amend to will be able to be reached or found or located. For this you are not responsible. If you can't locate someone, you are no longer responsible to make that amend. If you feel you need to make a symbolic amend, you may write them a letter and read it to them in a chair exercise. This symbolic amend may be helpful for you to resolve those issues.

List those people who, after trying, have not been able to be located.

1._____

2._____

3._____

4._____

5._____

Except

Except looks like the biggest word to some in this step. Many may think, "Oh good, a loophole." This is not what the word except means. This word except is used very sparingly. It means that there are some on the list that need to be exceptions. List those that you currently believe would be exceptions and to do so would cause them injury or harm to be aware of these issues now.

1._____

2._____

3._____

4._____

5._____

List five people you respect in recovery who have already done their Step Nine. Contact each of them and review your exception list and why you think they should be exceptions.

1._____

2._____

3._____

4._____

5._____

After talking to each of the persons listed above, what are their perceptions of whether your list of exceptions is appropriate? After considering their feedback, list those left that continue to be exempt.

1._____

2._____

3._____

4._____

5._____

What is the injury or harm that would be caused if you made an amend to those on your list above?

1._____

2._____

3._____

4._____

5._____

After prayer and meditation, do you have peace about these people not receiving a direct amend?

Yes _____   No _____

Make a list again of the people you owe amends to. In the column next to their name, list the date you made your amend. Caution: Do not wait, but actively pursue this!

Name   Date

1._____   _____

2._____   _____

3._____   _____

4._____   _____

5._____   _____

6._____   _____

7._____   _____

8._____   _____

9._____   _____

10._____   _____

11._____   _____

12._____   _____

13._____   _____

14._____   _____

15._____   _____

16._____   _____

17._____   _____

18._____   _____

19._____   _____

20._____   _____

How many direct amends can you make in the next week? Month? 3 Months?

     1 week _____   1 month _____   3 months _____

Complete your Step Nine by filling in the dates of all the people on this list. Your Step Nine is not completed until the last date is listed and all amends have been made.

What were some of your favorite conversations?_____

_____

_____

_____

_____

_____

_____

_____

What were some of the feelings you had before, during and after making your amends?

Before: I felt_____

During: I felt_____

After: I felt_____

How do you feel about these relationships after you made your amends?

I feel_____

_____

_____

I feel _____

_____

How do you feel about yourself now in the context of these relationships?

I feel _____

_____

I feel _____

_____

"Made direct amends to such people wherever possible, except when to do so would injure them or others." Do you feel you have fully experienced Step Nine? Why or why not?

_____

_____

_____

_____

What is the most significant thing you have learned about yourself in completing your Step Nine?

_____

_____

_____

_____

On a scale from 1-10 rate yourself on Step Nine.

1 2 3 4 5 6 7 8 9 10

Why? _____

_____

Feedback Form

The following space is provided for feedback ratings from your group in your step work. There is additional space as to why the rating is appropriate. You can use the feedback space also for reflection of your own work if you are working individually.

Name of Group Member _____ Rating 1 2 3 4 5 6 7 8 9 10

Feedback _____

_____

_____

Name of Group Member _____ Rating 1 2 3 4 5 6 7 8 9 10

Feedback _____

_____

_____

Name of Group Member _____ Rating 1 2 3 4 5 6 7 8 9 10

Feedback _____

_____

_____

Name of Group Member _____ Rating 1 2 3 4 5 6 7 8 9 10

Feedback _____

_____

_____

Name of Group Member _____ Rating 1 2 3 4 5 6 7 8 9 10

Feedback _____

_____

_____

Name of Group Member _____ Rating 1 2 3 4 5 6 7 8 9 10

Feedback _____

_____

_____

step ten

Continued to take personal inventory and when we
were wrong, promptly admitted it.

Continue

Continue is a process that will last a lifetime. Being human means making mistakes. Step Ten allows you a way of being human without accumulating guilt or shame from behavior or attitudes. Step Ten is a life-style. What is the date you are going to begin taking a daily personal inventory?

Date: _____/_____/_____

Personal Inventory

A personal inventory is a recording of what is in your person, both behaviors and attitudes. Both behavior and attitudes can hurt you as well as others. The other side of your inventory is strengths you have practiced today. Your recovery will promote your strengths toward growth. In Step Ten, don't proclaim your strengths to others. This is for you to know and to thank God for these strengths. Here, in Step Ten, you are being honest about your mistakes and then admitting them to those you made the mistake toward.

On the next page is a form to use over the next month to get you into a habit and also to make sure that this principle is being applied in your life. You are going to need to continue this process throughout your life. Now that you are shameless, you can relate to God and others more openly than ever before in your recovery.

Your personal inventory is not up at the end of the month. This form is only used to get you into a habit of being able to look honestly at yourself without shame and say, "that was a mistake" and admit it promptly. Remember that being human means we all make mistakes.

Day	Amends Asked For	Strength Acknowledged
1		
2		
3		
4		
5		
6		
7		
8		
9		
10		
11		
12		
13		
14		
15		
16		
17		
18		
19		
20		
21		
22		
23		
24		
25		
26		
27		
28		
29		
30		
31		

Promptly Admit It

Promptly means in a timely manner. It does not mean weeks or months later. It should not be much longer than the day you made this mistake. Admit it to yourself and the other person and move on. Within the above thirty-one days, how long did it take you to make your amends after you were aware you needed to? (Write in the time it took in the blank space next to "Day _____")

What is the average time it took you to make an amend? _____

Does the above time fit your definition for prompt?   Yes _____   No _____

If your answer is no, what is your plan to improve your promptness? Ask five people in the program who you know have done their Step Ten how they worked on promptness, record your findings below.

1. _____

2. _____

3. _____

4. _____

5. _____

"Continued to take personal inventory, and when we were wrong, promptly admitted it." Do you feel you have fully experienced Step Ten? Why or why not?

_____

_____

_____

_____

What is the most significant thing you have learned about yourself in completing your Step Ten?

_____

_____

_____

_____

On a scale from 1-10 rate yourself on Step Ten.

1 2 3 4 5 6 7 8 9 10

Why? _____
_____

Feedback Form

The following space is provided for feedback ratings from your group in your step work. There is additional space as to why the rating is appropriate. You can use the feedback space also for reflection of your own work if you are working individually.

Name of Group Member _____ Rating 1 2 3 4 5 6 7 8 9 10

Feedback _____

_____

_____

Name of Group Member _____ Rating 1 2 3 4 5 6 7 8 9 10

Feedback _____

_____

_____

Name of Group Member _____ Rating 1 2 3 4 5 6 7 8 9 10

Feedback _____

_____

_____

Name of Group Member _____ Rating 1 2 3 4 5 6 7 8 9 10

Feedback _____

_____

_____

Name of Group Member _____ Rating 1 2 3 4 5 6 7 8 9 10

Feedback _____

_____

_____

Name of Group Member _____ Rating 1 2 3 4 5 6 7 8 9 10

Feedback _____

_____

_____

step eleven

Sought through prayer and meditation to improve our conscious contact with God as we understood God, praying only for knowledge of God's will for us and the power to carry that out.

Sought

This means to seek with intentions to find. This takes effort and time.

Have you put time aside to pray and meditate on a regular basis?

Yes _____   No _____

If no, set aside time to do this daily. Once this time is set, you may or may not want to involve another person to make sure that you are accountable. If you choose to do this, what is the person's name?

_____

Check off what you were able to do on a daily basis for the next month.

Day	Prayer	Meditation	Day	Prayer	Meditation
1			17		
2			18		
3			19		
4			20		
5			21		
6			22		
7			23		
8			24		
9			25		
10			26		
11			27		
12			28		
13			29		
14			30		
15			31		
16					

Conscious Contact

What have been some of your "contact" experiences with God over the past month?

_____

_____

_____

_____

_____

_____

_____

_____

_____

_____

Some people journal their contacts with God. Would you like to make that a part of your spiritual life?

Yes _____   No _____

Knowledge of His Will

Another question to ask yourself is, "am I praying for the knowledge of His will?" If you are doing this, put a "Y" next to the days you pray.

What knowledge of His will have you gained over the past month?

_____

_____

_____

_____

_____

_____

_____

_____

_____

_____

Over the past month, in what way has God given you the power to carry out His will as you have understood it? Be specific.

_____

_____

_____

_____

This format was designed only to get you into the habit of being consciously aware that you are praying and meditating to improve your contact with God. This is a great way of living a shameless relationship with God and others. Spirituality will continue to be important as you walk through your healing process.

"Sought through prayer and meditation to improve our conscious contact with God as we understand Him praying only for the knowledge of His will for us and the power to carry that out." Do you feel you have fully experienced Step Eleven? Why or why not?

_____

_____

_____

_____

What is the most significant thing you have learned about yourself in completing your Step Eleven?

_____

_____

_____

_____

On a scale from 1-10 rate yourself on Step Eleven.

1 2 3 4 5 6 7 8 9 10

Why? _____

_____

Feedback Form

The following space is provided for feedback ratings from your group in your step work. There is additional space as to why the rating is appropriate. You can use the feedback space also for reflection of your own work if you are working individually.

Name of Group Member _____ Rating 1 2 3 4 5 6 7 8 9 10

Feedback _____

_____

_____

Name of Group Member _____ Rating 1 2 3 4 5 6 7 8 9 10

Feedback _____

_____

_____

Name of Group Member _____ Rating 1 2 3 4 5 6 7 8 9 10

Feedback _____

_____

_____

Name of Group Member _____ Rating 1 2 3 4 5 6 7 8 9 10

Feedback _____

_____

_____

Name of Group Member _____ Rating 1 2 3 4 5 6 7 8 9 10

Feedback _____

_____

_____

Name of Group Member _____ Rating 1 2 3 4 5 6 7 8 9 10

Feedback _____

_____

_____

step twelve

Having had a spiritual awakening as the results of these steps,
we tried to carry this message to others and to practice these
principles in all our day-to-day living.

Having Had A Spiritual Awakening

In many ways, recovery has brought you several awakenings, all of which are spiritual.

What were some of the awakenings that you have had in your spiritual life since you have started your recovery?

_____

_____

_____

_____

_____

_____

_____

_____

What part of this awakening was a direct result of working the steps?_____

_____

_____

_____

What steps seemed to be important to you as far as a spiritual awakening? _____

_____

_____

_____

_____

Tried to Carry This Message to Others

How have you tried to carry this message during your healing process?_____

_____

_____

How do you intend to carry this message from here on?_____

_____

_____

What are some things you have learned about yourself and others as you have carried the message to others? _____

_____

_____

What are some experiences you have had in "giving it away?"_____

_____

_____

How did you feel after "giving it away" in the above incidents?

I feel_____

_____

I feel_____

_____

And To Practice These Principles In All Our Day To Day Living

The principles of honesty, spirituality, and being responsible for your own behavior, good or bad, and being prompt about admitting it, are all important. This is especially true as you continue to live a life-style of healing so that you do not carry guilt and shame that could bring you back into an unhealthy place. You deserve the best healthy life-style you could ever have. In giving it away, you will find that your own recovery is enhanced.

Identify below how have you practiced these principles in your:

Spiritual life?

1._____

_____

2._____

_____

3._____

_____

Emotional life?

1._____

_____

2._____

_____

3._____

_____

Social life?

1._____

_____

2._____

_____

3._____

_____

Taking care of your health/body?

1._____

_____

2._____

_____

3._____
_____

Financial life?

1._____
_____

2._____
_____

3._____
_____

Parenting?

1._____
_____

2._____
_____

3._____
_____

Work relationships?

1._____
_____

2._____
_____

3._____
_____

Your parents?

1._____
_____

2. _____

_____

3. _____

_____

Sexuality?

1. _____

_____

2. _____

_____

3. _____

_____

Significant relationships?

1. _____

_____

2. _____

_____

3. _____

_____

"Having had a spiritual awakening as the result of these steps, we tried to carry this message to others and to practice these principles in all our day to day living." Do you feel you have fully experienced Step Twelve? Why or why not?

_____

_____

_____

_____

What is the most significant thing you learned about yourself completing Step Twelve?

_____

_____

_____

_____

On a scale from 1-10 rate yourself on Step Twelve.

1 2 3 4 5 6 7 8 9 10

Why? _____

_____

Feedback Form

The following space is provided for feedback ratings from your group in your step work. There is additional space as to why the rating is appropriate. You can use the feedback space also for reflection of your own work if you are working individually.

Name of Group Member _____Rating 1   2   3   4   5   6   7   8   9   10

Feedback _____

_____

_____

Name of Group Member _____Rating 1   2   3   4   5   6   7   8   9   10

Feedback _____

_____

_____

Name of Group Member _____Rating 1   2   3   4   5   6   7   8   9   10

Feedback _____

_____

_____

Name of Group Member _____Rating 1   2   3   4   5   6   7   8   9   10

Feedback _____

_____

_____

Name of Group Member _____Rating 1   2   3   4   5   6   7   8   9   10

Feedback _____

_____

_____

Name of Group Member _____Rating 1   2   3   4   5   6   7   8   9   10

Feedback _____

_____

_____

Appendix

Feelings Exercise

1. I feel (put feeling word here) when (put a present situation when you feel this).

2. I first remember feeling (put the same feeling word here) when (explain earliest occurrence of this feeling).

Abandoned	Battered	Considerate	Distrusted	Goofy
Abused	Beaten	Consumed	Disturbed	Grateful
Aching	Beautiful	Content	Dominated	Greedy
Accepted	Belligerent	Cool	Domineering	Grief
Accused	Belittled	Courageous	Doomed	Grim
Accepting	Bereaved	Courteous	Doubtful	Grimy
Admired	Betrayed	Coy	Dreadful	Grouchy
Adored	Bewildered	Crabby	Eager	Grumpy
Adventurous	Blamed	Cranky	Ecstatic	Hard
Affectionate	Blaming	Crazy	Edgy	Harried
Agony	Bonded	Creative	Edified	Hassled
Alienated	Bored	Critical	Elated	Healthy
Aloof	Bothered	Criticized	Embarrassed	Helpful
Aggravated	Brave	Cross	Empowered	Helpless
Agreeable	Breathless	Crushed	Empty	Hesitant
Aggressive	Bristling	Cuddly	Enraged	High
Alive	Broken-up	Curious	Enraptured	Hollow
Alone	Bruised	Cut	Enthusiastic	Honest
Alluring	Bubbly	Damned	Enticed	Hopeful
Amazed	Burdened	Dangerous	Esteemed	Hopeless
Amused	Burned	Daring	Exasperated	Horrified
Angry	Callous	Dead	Excited	Hostile
Anguished	Calm	Deceived	Exhilarated	Humiliated
Annoyed	Capable	Deceptive	Exposed	Hurried
Anxious	Captivated	Defensive	Fake	Hurt
Apart	Carefree	Delicate	Fascinated	Hyper
Apathetic	Careful	Delighted	Feisty	Ignorant
Apologetic	Careless	Demeaned	Ferocious	Ignored
Appreciated	Caring	Demoralized	Foolish	Immature
Appreciative	Cautious	Dependent	Forced	Impatient
Apprehensive	Certain	Depressed	Forceful	Important
Appropriate	Chased	Deprived	Forgiven	Impotent
Approved	Cheated	Deserted	Forgotten	Impressed
Argumentative	Cheerful	Desirable	Free	Incompetent
Aroused	Childlike	Desired	Friendly	Incomplete
Astonished	Choked-up	Despair	Frightened	Independent
Assertive	Close	Despondent	Frustrated	Insecure
Attached	Cold	Destroyed	Full	Innocent
Attacked	Comfortable	Different	Funny	Insignificant
Attentive	Comforted	Dirty	Furious	Insincere
Attractive	Competent	Disenchanted	Gay	Isolated
Aware	Competitive	Disgusted	Generous	Inspired
Awestruck	Complacent	Disinterested	Gentle	Insulted
Badgered	Complete	Dispirited	Genuine	Interested
Baited	Confident	Distressed	Giddy	Intimate
Bashful	Confused	Distrustful	Giving	Intolerant

Involved
Irate
Irrational
Irked
Irresponsible
Irritable
Irritated
Isolated
Jealous
Jittery
Joyous
Lively
Lonely
Loose
Lost
Loving
Low
Lucky
Lustful
Mad
Maudlin
Malicious
Mean
Miserable
Misunderstood
Moody
Morose
Mournful
Mystified
Nasty
Nervous
Nice
Numb
Nurtured
Nuts
Obsessed
Offended
Open
Ornery
Out of control
Overcome
Overjoyed
Overpowered
Overwhelmed
Pampered
Panicked
Paralyzed
Paranoid
Patient
Peaceful

Pensive
Perceptive
Perturbed
Phony
Pleasant
Pleased
Positive
Powerless
Present
Precious
Pressured
Pretty
Proud
Pulled apart
Put down
Puzzled
Quarrelsome
Queer
Quiet
Raped
Ravished
Ravishing
Real
Refreshed
Regretful
Rejected
Rejuvenated
Rejecting
Relaxed
Relieved
Remarkable
Remembered
Removed
Repulsed
Repulsive
Resentful
Resistant
Responsible
Responsive
Repressed
Respected
Restless
Revolved
Riled
Rotten
Ruined
Sad
Safe
Satiated
Satisfied

Scared
Scolded
Scorned
Scrutinized
Secure
Seduced
Seductive
Self-centered
Self-conscious
Selfish
Separated
Sensuous
Sexy
Shattered
Shocked
Shot down
Shy
Sickened
Silly
Sincere
Sinking
Smart
Smothered
Smug
Sneaky
Snowed
Soft
Solid
Solitary
Sorry
Spacey
Special
Spiteful
Spontaneous
Squelched
Starved
Stiff
Stimulated
Stifled
Strangled
Strong
Stubborn
Stuck
Stunned
Stupid
Subdued
Submissive
Successful
Suffocated
Sure

Sweet
Sympathy
Tainted
Tearful
Tender
Tense
Terrific
Terrified
Thrilled
Ticked
Tickled
Tight
Timid
Tired
Tolerant
Tormented
Torn
Tortured
Touched
Trapped
Tremendous
Tricked
Trusted
Trustful
Trusting
Ugly
Unacceptable
Unapproach-
able
Unaware
Uncertain
Uncomfortable
Under control
Understanding
Understood
Undesirable
Unfriendly
Ungrateful
Unified
Unhappy
Unimpressed
Unsafe
Unstable
Upset
Uptight
Used
Useful
Useless
Unworthy
Validated

Valuable
Valued
Victorious
Violated
Violent
Voluptuous
Vulnerable
Warm
Wary
Weak
Whipped
Whole
Wicked
Wild
Willing
Wiped out
Wishful
Withdrawn
Wonderful
Worried
Worthy
Wounded
Young
Zapped

The Twelve Steps of Alcoholics Anonymous

1. We admitted we were powerless over alcohol--that our lives had become unmanageable.

2. Came to believe that a Power greater than ourselves could restore us to sanity.

3. Made a decision to turn our will and our lives over to the care of God as we understood Him.

4. Made a searching and fearless moral inventory of ourselves.

5. Admitted to God, to ourselves, and to another human being the exact nature of our wrongs.

6. Were entirely ready to have God remove all these defects of character.

7. Humbly asked Him to remove our shortcomings.

8. Made a list of all people we had harmed, and became willing to make amends to them all.

9. Made direct amends to such people wherever possible, except when to do so would injure them or others.

10. Continued to take personal inventory, and when we were wrong, promptly admitted it.

11. Sought through prayer and meditation to improve our conscious contact with God as we understood Him, praying only for knowledge of His will for us and the power to carry that out.

12. Having had a spiritual awakening as the result of these steps, we tried to carry this message to others and to practice these principles in all our affairs.

The Twelve Steps of Alcoholics Anonymous Adapted for Partners

1. We admitted we were powerless over our partner's sexual addiction, and that our lives had become unmanageable.

2. Came to believe that a Power greater than ourselves could restore us to sanity.

3. Made a decision to turn our will and our lives over to the care of God as we understood Him.

4. Made a searching and fearless moral inventory of ourselves.

5. Admitted to God, to ourselves, and to another human being the exact nature of our wrongs.

6. Were entirely ready to have God remove all these defects of character.

7. Humbly asked Him to remove our shortcomings.

8. Made a list of all people we had harmed, and became willing to make amends to them all.

9. Made direct amends to such people wherever possible, except when to do so would injure them or others.

10. Continued to take personal inventory, and when we were wrong, promptly admitted it.

11. Sought through prayer and meditation to improve our conscious contact with God as we understood Him, praying only for knowledge of His will for us and the power to carry that out.

12. Having had a spiritual awakening as the result of these steps, we tried to carry this message to others and to practice these principles in all our affairs.

PRODUCTS FOR PARTNER'S RECOVERY

Partners: Healing From His Addiction

$14.95

Partners: Healing from His Addiction offers real hope that you can heal from his sexual addictions. After presenting statistics and personal stories, it will walk you down the path to reclaim your life, your voice, and your power, to be who you are without the impact of his addiction.

Partners Recovery Guide: 100 Empowering Exercises

$39.95

The *Partners Recovery Guide : 100 Empowering Exercises* guide was borne out of the latest in Christian self help books research on the effects on a woman who has lived with a sexual addict. This workbook will take you down the clear path of healing from the devastating impact of his sex addiction and accompany you along your entire journey.

Beyond Love: A 12 Step Guide for Partners

$14.95

Beyond Love is an interactive workbook that allows the partners of sex addicts to gain insight and strength through working the Twelve Steps. This book can be used for individual purposes or as a group study workbook.

Partner Betrayal Trauma

BOOK:$22.95/DVD:$65.95

Partner Betrayal Trauma will help you unlock that power by providing an outstanding guide on how to become stronger every day and get past the trauma of betrayal. The pain and experience of betrayal impacts all of your being and relationships. Fix your broken heart, help your relationships, and reclaim your marriage with the necessary strategies for your personal recovery.

Partner Betrayal Trauma: The Workbook

$39.95

In this workbook by Dr. Weiss, you will gain the insight and support you need to understand what betrayal trauma is and how to overcome it to be the strongest version of yourself. This is an excellent guide for those struggling to overcome the past trauma of a betrayal in their relationship.

Partner Betrayal Trauma: Step Guide

$14.95

This is an excellent step-by-step guide for those struggling to overcome the past trauma of a betrayal in their relationship. You will gain insight from a therapist who has worked with countless patients and families for over 30 years to provide them with the support they need to come out the other side whole and better versions of themselves.

He Needs To Change, Dr. Weiss

$29.95

He Needs To Change, Dr. Weiss DVD addresses the pain, trauma, and betrayal women experience because of their partner's sex addiction, betrayal, and/or intimacy anorexia. In this DVD, Dr. Weiss addresses the issue of change that he has explained to thousands of women in his office.

Unstuck for Partners

$29.95

The *Unstuck* DVD is for every woman who has experienced the pain of their partner's sex addiction or intimacy anorexia and feels stuck, confused, frustrated and unable to move on. You didn't sign up for this and honestly, you don't get it! This DVD helps you "get it" so you can process the painful reality you are in and start to live again.

Why Do I Stay, When it Doesn't make Sense

$39.95

In this video, Dr. Doug Weiss utilizes his several decades of experience to give you information and tools that can help you make your decision with mental clarity and confidence. Whether you decide to stay, separate, or divorce, your future can be filled with new opportunities and a life that you genuinely enjoy.

Triggered

$49.00

In the Triggered DVD, Dr. Weiss gives women a repertoire of tools to be successful when a trigger occurs. Triggers are normal for partners of sex addicts, but each woman's triggers are unique and must be navigated in different ways. This DVD can be a life-changing message which will validate your struggles to heal and help you face the challenges of being triggered after partner betrayal trauma.

PRODUCTS FOR INTIMACY ANOREXIA

Helping My Spouse Heal from My Intimacy Anorexia Video Course

$99.00

Are you struggling to validate your spouse's pain from Intimacy Anorexia and help them begin to heal? For the spouse of an intimacy anorexic, the pain is excruciating and sometimes even debilitating. This course is for the intimacy anorexic who is aware of their behaviors and wants to transition into a connected, intimate relationship with their spouse.

Intimacy Anorexia

BOOK:$22.95/DVD:$69.95

This hidden addiction is destroying so many marriages today. In your hands is the first antidote for someone with intimacy anorexia to turn the pages on this addiction process. Excerpts from intimacy anorexics and their spouses help this book become clinically helpful and personal in its impact to communicate hope and healing for the intimacy anorexic and the marriage.

Intimacy Anorexia: The Workbook

$39.95

Intimacy Anorexia is a hidden addiction that is destryoing many marriages today. Within the pages of this workbook you will find more than 100 practical and empowering exercises to guide you through your personal recovery towards intimacy. Douglas Weiss has been successfully counseling intimacy anorexics for many years in his practice.

Intimacy Anorexia: The Steps

$14.95

This workbook follows in the tradition of the Twelve-Steps breaking down the various principles for readers so that they can experience freedom from intimacy anorexia. It is our hope that you will join the millions who have received help in their personal recovery using these Twelve-Steps.

Pain for Love

$29.95

Pain For Love describes in detail one of the most insidious strategies of an intimacy anorexic with their spouse. This dynamic is experienced by many who are married to an intimacy anorexic. This paradigm can empower the spouse and help them stop participating in a pain for love dynamic in their marriage.

Sin of Withholding

$49.95

This DVD is the first to address the Biblical foundation of the sin of withholding in believers' hearts. The practical application in marriage addressing Intimacy Anorexia is also interwoven in this revelational teaching on the Sin of Withholding. Once a believer is free of this sin, their walk with the Lord and their fruit towards others can increase expediently.

Narcissism Sex Addiction & Intimacy Anorexia

$29.95

The profound information that you will learn in this DVD will help you fairly evaluate your specific situation for narcissism, which will help you develop a treatment plan to address the issue you are dealing with at its core. Having this clarity can help expedite the healing process for the sex addict, intimacy anorexic, and the spouse, as they are able to tackle the real issue at hand.

Married and Alone

BOOK:$14.95/DVD:$49.95

The impact of being married and alone is very real. Dr. Weiss explains why and will help you to start a journey of recovery from living with a spouse with intimacy or sexual anorexia. My hope is that whatever reason you are watching this DVD you realize that you are worthy of being loved, whether your spouse has decided to pursue recovery or has chosen his or her anorexia over you.

Married and Alone: Healing Exercises for Spouses

$39.95

This workbook is designed to help the spouse heal from the impact of their relationship with an intimacy anorexic which may have been experienced over years or decades. The addiction patterns of an alcoholic, gambler, overeater, sex addict or intimacy anorexic have a direct impact on their spouse's life in so many ways.

Married and Alone: The Twelve Step Guide

$14.95

This book follows in the tradition of the Twelve-Steps by breaking down the various principles for each reader so that they can experience the discovery of the Twelve-Step promises. It is our hope that you will join the millions who have received help in their recovery by using these Twelve-Steps. These Steps can further your healing and recovery from your spouse's Intimacy Anorexia.

PRODUCTS FOR MEN'S RECOVERY

The Final Freedom

BOOK: $22.95/$35.00

The Final Freedom gives more current information than many professional counselors have today. In addition to informing sex addicts and their partners about sex addiction, it gives hope for recovery. The information provided in this book would cost hundreds of dollars in counseling hours to receive. Many have attested to successful recovery from this information alone.

101 Freedom Exercises

$39.95

This workbook provides tips, principles, survival techniques and therapeutic homework that has been tested and proven on many recovering sex addicts from all walks of life who have practiced these principles and have maintained their sobriety for many years. Jesus promised us a life of freedom, this book makes this promise a practical journey.

Steps to Freedom

$14.95

The Twelve Steps of recovery have become a major influence in the restoration of this country from the age old problem of alcohol and substance abuse. This book follows in the tradition of the Twelve Steps from a Christian perspective breaking down the various principles for each reader so that they can experience the freedom from sexual addiction.

Partner Betrayal Trauma

DVD:$69.95/COMPANION GUIDE:$11.95

The *Helping Her Heal* DVD paired with this companion guide are both vital tools for the man who has struggled with sexual addiction, exposed his marriage to the fallout of betrayal by acting on his urges, and is now seeking how to help his wife heal from the trauma of this devastating discovery.

Disclosure: Preparing and Completing

$39.95

This information can help the addict and the spouse navigate these often uncharted and misguided waters, saving the addict and the spouse from unnecessary pain or trauma. This DVD can expedite the understanding of each of the significant processes of disclosure for the addict, the spouse, and the marriage.

Healing Her Heart After Relapse

$29.95

This DVD is way more than, "He relapses, he does a consequence and moves on." The addict is given real tools to address the emotional damage and repair of her heart as a result of a relapse. Every couple in recovery would do well to have these tools before a potential relapse.

Boundaries: His. Hers.Ours

$49.95

Boundaries are a healthy, normal, and necessary part of the recovery process for sex addicts, intimacy anorexics, and their spouses. Implementing boundaries in a relationship may seem difficult, but with the proper tools and guidance you can successfully introduce and implement boundaries in your relationship. In this DVD set, Dr. Doug Weiss provides an answer to the clarion call on boundaries by educating and guiding you through this process.

Marriage After Addiction

$29.95

Addiction can have devastating effects on even good marriages. In this DVD you are intelligently guided through the journey you will experience if addiction is part of your marriage story. You will learn important information about the early and later stages of recovery for your marriage.

Series For Men

Clean: A Proven Plan For Men Committed to Sexual Integrity

BOOK: $16.95/DVD:$29.95/JOURNAL:$14.95

Clean is a priceless, no-nonsense resource for every husband, father, brother, son, friend, pastor, and Christian leader on the front lines of this war. It is a soldier's handbook for those ready to reclaim their homes, churches, and nations for the God who has built them to succeed.

Lust Free Living

BOOK:$13.95/DVD:$23.95

Every man can fight for and obtain a lust free lifestyle. Once you know how to stop lust, you will realize how weak lust really can be. God gace you the power to protect those you love from the ravages of lust for the rest of your life! It's time to take it back!

Men Make Men

DVD:$29.95/GUIDEBOOK:$11.95

Dr. Weiss takes the listeners by the hand and step-by-step walks through the creative process God used to make every man into a man of God. This practical teaching on DVD combined with the Men Make Guidebook can revitalize the men in any home or local church.

Addiction Recovery

Recovery for Everyone

BOOK: $22.95/DVD:$99.00/WORKBOOK:$39.95/STEPBOOK: $14.95

Recovery for Everyone helps addicts fight and recover from any addiction they are facing. Learn truths and gain a biblical understanding to break the strongholds in your life.

You will also find an explanation as to how an addiction may have become a part of your life and details as to how you can walk the path to recovery. You will find a roadmap to help you begin and navigate an incredible journey toward freedom. Then you can become part of the solution and even help others get free as well.

Secret Solutions: More Than 100 Ways to End the Secret

$39.95

Female sexual addiction is real and impacting many women's lives today. This Workbook is a practical step-by-step guide for recovery from this growing issue in our culture. The *Secret Solutions*, can be used in conjunction with therapy or as part of Twelve Step relationships or groups you may be a part of. My hope is that you receive the precious gift of recovery as many others have, and that you maintain it the rest of your life, for your benefit and for the benefit of those you love.

Marriage Resources

Lover Spouse

$13.95

This book provides guidelines to lead a prosperous married life and is helpful for anyone wanting to know more about what the Lord Almighty desires for your love and marriage. Featured with practical tips and foundational relationship skills, the information offered in this book will guide couples through the process of creating an intimate Christian marriage based on a solid biblical worldview.

Upgrade Your Sex Life

BOOK:$16.95/DVD:$29.95

Upgrade Your Sex Life actually teaches you own unique sexual expression that you and your partner are pre-wired to enjoy. Once you learn what your type is, you can communicate and have sex on a more satisfying level.

Servant Marriage

$13.95

Servant Marriage book is a Revelation on God's Masterpiece of marriage. In these pages, you will walk with God as He creates the man, the woman and his masterpiece called marriage.

Marriage Mondays

$59.95

This is an eight week marriage training that actually gives you the skills to have a healthy, more vibrant marriage. Each week Dr. Weiss tackles major aspects of marriage from a biblical perspective. Apply these techniques and it will transform your marriage. This course provides couples to grow their marriages either in a small group setting or as their very own private marriage retreat.

Intimacy: 100 Day Guide to a Lasting Relationship

$11.99

The *Intimacy: A 100 Day Guide to Lasting Relationships* book gives you a game plan to improve your relationships. Intimacy doesn't need to be illusive! It's time to recognize intimacy for what it is – a loving and lifelong process that you can learn and develop.

Other Resources

Worthy

WORKBOOK: $29.95/DVD$29.95

The Worthy Workbook and DVD, is designed for a 12 week study. Here is a path that anyone can take to get and stay worthy. Follow this path, and you too will make the journey from worthless to worthy just as others have.

Emotional Fitness

$16.95

Everyone has an unlimited number of emotions, but few have been trained to identify, choose, communicate, and master them. More than a guide for gaining emotional fitness and mastery, in these pages you will find a pathway to a much more fulfilling life.

Letters to My Daughter

$14.95

A gift for your daughter as she enters college. Letters to my Daughter includes my daily letters to my daughter during her first year of college. The letters are about life, God, boys, relationships and being successful in college and life in general.

Born for War

$29.95

Born for War teaches practical tools to defeat these sexual landmines and offers scriptural truths that empower young men to desire successfulness in the war thrust upon them. In this DVD, he equips this generation to win the war for their destiny. It also includes one session for parents to support their son through this battle.

Princes Take Longer Than Frogs

$29.95

This 2 hour DVD helps single women ages 15-30, to successfully navigate through the season of dating. Dr. Weiss' *Princes Take Longer Than Frogs* is a faith-based discussion broken up into several segments including Characteristics of Princes and Frogs, lies women Believe, Dating, Accountability, Boundaries, Sex and the Brain and so much more.

Indestructible

$29.95

The Indestructible series gives you a foundational understanding about your innate design as God's child. Addiction, betrayal, and abuse or neglected can all cause trials in our lives that can trigger feelings of worthlessness and defeat. God's Word reveals that your soul is not capable of being destroyed. Once you recognize and embrace your indestructible nature, you can change how you think, feel, and believe about your past, present, and future!

Sex after Recovery

$59.95

Sex after Recovery will help you navigate a variety of issues including how to reclaim a healthy sexual life together. This DVD set will help you to reclaim and recover your sexuality both individually and with each other.

Sexual Templates

$29.95

Dr. Doug Weiss, a Licensed Psychologist who has worked with thousands of men and women who are sexually addicted, have experienced trauma, or have had negative sexual experiences which have impacted their sexual template, will use his thirty years experience to help you rewire your brain and recreate a new, relational sexual template with your spouse.

I Need to Feel Safe
$29.95

This DVD provides a clear path to processing your desire for safety and creates a roadmap to reclaim safety regardless of your partner or spouse's choices. Dr. Weiss has helped thousands of women rebuild their fractured safety, heal the betrayal, and find hope for themselves. If your heart has cried out to feel safe, this DVD is a response to that heart cry.

Intrigue Addiction:

$29.95

The intrigue addict is constantly on the hunt for a look or gesture from another person that insinuates they are attracted to or interested in them. The intrigue addiction can go unnoticed, but it can create just as much pain for the spouse as other sexually addictive behaviors.

Prodigal Parent Process Resources

Prodigal Parent Process
BOOK: $19.95/DVD$59.95

Dr. Weiss, drawing upon his thirty-plus years of experience working with prodigals and parents of prodigals, delivers biblical and practical tools to aid you in your journey to hope and healing. You can't change the fact that you have a prodigal but you can set your mind upon how you will go through this journey with your prodigal.

Prodigal Parent Process Workbook
$16.95

In conjunction with the Parent Prodigal Process videos and book, this workbook helps you therapeutically work through deep-rooted struggles related to being a parent of a prodigal. Working through this series and workbook will prompt serious internal dialogue with yourself as it relates to your prodigal child.

Counseling Services

"Without the intensive, my marriage would have ended and I would not have known why. Now I am happier than ever and my marriage is bonded permanently."

Counseling Sessions

Couples are helped through critical phases of disclosure moving into the process of recovery, and rebuilding trust in relationships. We have helped many couples rebuild their relationship and grasp and implement the necessary skills for an intimate relationship.

Individual counseling offers a personal treatment plan for successful healing in your life. In just one session a counselor can help you understand how you became stuck and how to move toward freedom.

Partners of sex addicts need an advocate. Feelings of fear, hurt, anger, betrayal, and grief require a compassionate, effective response. We provide that expert guidance and direction. We have helped many partners heal through sessions that get them answers to their many questions including: "How can I trust him again?"

A counseling session today can begin your personal journey toward healing.

3 and 5 Day Intensives

in Colorado Springs, Colorado are available for the following issues:

- Sexual Addiction Couple or Individual
- Intimacy Anorexia
- Partners of Sexual Addicts
- Partner Betrayal Trauma

Attendees of Intensives will receive:

- Personal attention from counselors who specialize in your area of need
- An understanding of how the addiction /anorexia and its consequences came into being
- Three appointments daily
- Daily assignments to increase the productiveness of these daily sessions
- Individuals get effective counseling to recover from the effects of sexual addiction, abuse and anorexia
- Addiction, abuse, anorexia issues are thoroughly addressed for couples and individuals. This includes the effects on the partner or family members of the addict, and how to rebuild intimacy toward a stronger relationship.

A·A·S·A·T

American Association for Sex Addiction Therapy

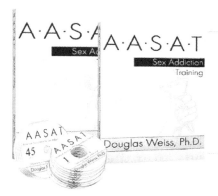

Sex Addiction Training Set

$1195

Both men and women are seeking to counsel more than ever for sexually addictive behaviors. You can be prepared! Forty-seven hours of topics related to sexual addiction treatment are covered in this training including:
- The Six Types of Sex Addicts
- Neurological Understanding
- Sex and Recovery
- Relapse Strategies

Partner's Recovery Training Set

$995

With this AASAT training, you will gain proven clinical insight into treating the issues facing partners. You can be prepared! Thirty-nine hours of topics related to partners treatment are covered in this training, including:
- Partner Model
- Partner Grief
- Anger
- Boundaries

Intimacy Anorexia Training Set

$995

This growing issue of Intimacy Anorexia will need your competent help in your community. Now, you can be prepared to identify it and treat it. In this training you'll cover topics like:
- Identifying Intimacy Anorexia
- Causes of Intimacy Anorexia
- Treatment Plan
- Relapse Strategies

For more information visit www.aasat.org or call 719.330.2425

Struggling with Trauma, Anxiety, and PTSD?

Trauma, anxiety, and PTSD can imbalance your brain. When your brain is out of balance, or stuck, you don't feel right and it's impossible to function at your highest level. Cereset is a proven technology that's non-invasive and highly effective. Cereset can help your brain free itself, enabling you to achieve higher levels of well-being and balance throughout your life.

Cereset – Garden of the Gods is located at Heart to Heart Counseling Center in Colorado Springs, Colorado and specializes in working with sexual addiction, intimacy anorexia, betrayal trauma, PTSD, anxiety, and more.

Here's what clients had to say about Cereset Garden of the Gods after their sessions:

"Cereset helped save our marriage. My husband and I both did Cereset and with it helping both of us be calmer and sleep better, we respond to each other in a more loving and respectful way. I notice a big change in him, and he says the same about me. After the sessions I noticed a marked improvement in my sleep and my ability to stay calm during moments that would trigger an argument with my spouse prior to Cereset. Before Cereset we felt chaotic and now, afterwards, we both feel more at peace. our household is a is a calm place to be now and we are so grateful!"

"I've noticed a significant improvement in my ability to control and correct my patterns of thought – specifically negative thoughts. I also noticed my reaction to negative events was calmer and more controlled instead of being thrown in a downward spiral. I'm more able to recognize and deal with stress."

"As a health care provider, I would refer patients for Cereset. I suffered from extreme sleeplessness; difficulty falling asleep and staying asleep. I did not sleep more than 2-3 hours a night for years. By the week's end I slept 7 hours a night! I also suffered from extreme anxiety and PTSD, which after years led to depression and feelings of hopelessness/helplessness. My anxiety has significantly improved. You were amazing, professional, knowledgeable, and tailored to my needs very well. Cereset produces results. If you are on the fence about this, trust the evidence-based studies and the thousands of positive testimonials. You will NOT regret it."

View a client testimonial here

Schedule Your Cereset Intensive Today!

The cost for five sessions (one per day) is $1,500.

For more information call us at 719-644-5778

Made in the USA
Middletown, DE
18 October 2022

12928704R00077